W9-DDZ-684

ATHENA

B. A. Hoena

Consultant:
Dr. Laurel Bowman
Department of Greek and Roman Studies
University of Victoria, British Columbia

Capstone
press
Mankato, Minnesota

Capstone Press
151 Good Counsel Drive, P.O. Box 669, Mankato, Minnesota 56002
http://www.capstonepress.com

Library of Congress Cataloging-in-Publication Data
Hoena, B. A.
    Athena / B.A. Hoena.
    p. cm.—(World mythology)
    Summary: Relates the exploits of Athena and her importance in Greek mythology, including her connection to such figures as Jason and Odysseus, and describes the role of myths in the modern world.
    Includes bibliographical references and index.
    ISBN 0-7368-3453-2 (paperback) ISBN 0-7368-1608-9 (hardcover)
    1. Athena (Greek deity)—Juvenile literature. [1. Athena (Greek deity) 2. Mythology, Greek.] I. Title. II. Series.
BL820.M6 H64 2003
292.2'114—dc21
                                                      2002008461

Editorial Credits
Karen Risch, product planning editor; Juliette Peters, book designer and illustrator;
    Alta Schaffer, photo researcher

Photo Credits
Art Resource/Giraudon, 4; Réunion des Musées Nationaux, 8, 10, 18
Corbis/Mimmo Jodice, cover; National Gallery Collection; By kind permission of the
    Trustees of the National Gallery, London, 12; Alexander Burkatowski, 14; Peter M.
    Wilson, 20
Sally Gray photography, 16

1 2 3 4 5 6 08 07 06 05 04 03

TABLE OF CONTENTS

This Greek statue shows Athena holding an owl. Owls were one of her symbols. People thought owls were wise like Athena. "Wise as an owl" is a saying to describe a smart person.

ATHENA

In Greek myths, Athena (uh-THEE-nuh) was the goddess of wisdom and courage. She also was the goddess of useful arts. These crafts included weaving, farming, cooking, and playing music. Athena was known as Minerva (mi-NER-vuh) in Roman myths.

Unlike other gods, Athena was not quick to anger. She believed it was better to settle arguments with wisdom rather than fighting. But Athena did encourage people to fight wisely and for a good cause.

Athena was the protector of heroes. She helped mythical people like Jason, Hercules (HUR-kyoo-leez), and Odysseus (oh-DISS-ee-uhss). Athena gave these heroes advice or gifts to help them on their adventures.

Athena was one of the 12 Olympians. Ancient Greeks and Romans believed these powerful gods ruled the world from Mount Olympus. This mountain is in central Greece. Ancient people believed the gods controlled every part of their lives.

GREEK and ROMAN Mythical Figures

Greek Name: **ATHENA**
Roman Name: **MINERVA**
Zeus' daughter and goddess
of wisdom

Greek Name: **HEPHAESTUS**
Roman Name: **VULCAN**
Zeus' son and god of fire

Greek Name: **HERACLES**
Roman Name: **HERCULES**
Greek hero famous for performing
his 12 labors

Greek Name: **NIKE**
Roman Name: **VICTORIA**
Goddess of victory

Greek Name: **ODYSSEUS**
Roman Name: **ULYSSES**
Greek hero whose adventures are
told in Homer's *The Odyssey*

Greek Name: **POSEIDON**
Roman Name: **NEPTUNE**
Zeus' brother and god of the sea

Greek Name: **PROMETHEUS**
Roman Name: **PROMETHEUS**
Titan who created animals and gave
people the gift of fire

Greek Name: **ZEUS**
Roman Name: **JUPITER**
Athena's father and ruler of
the Olympians

ABOUT MYTHOLOGY

The word myth comes from the Greek word *mythos*. This word means tale or story. Mythology is a collection of stories.

Ancient Greeks and Romans used myths to help them understand the world. They did not know how to explain nature using science. They did not know why things like earthquakes or storms happened. Ancient Greeks and Romans told stories to explain these events.

The myth of Arachne (uh-RAK-nee) explained why spiders weave webs. Arachne was a skilled weaver. Athena became angry with her and turned her into a spider. As a spider, Arachne kept her skill of weaving by making webs.

Myths also explained the source of objects. Ancient Greeks believed Athena made flutes and trumpets so people could play music. They believed Athena made rakes and plows so people could grow crops. Myths also say that Athena invented the loom. People use this machine to weave cloth.

Rene Antoine Houasse painted this scene of Athena's birth. Zeus lies in the center of the painting as Athena leaps from his head. Hephaestus is next to Zeus and holds an ax.

THE BIRTH OF ATHENA

Athena was the daughter of Zeus (ZOOSS). Zeus ruled the Olympians. The Titaness Metis (ME-tiss) was Athena's mother.

Zeus received a warning while Metis was pregnant with Athena. His grandmother told him that Metis' second child would be a son. This son would be strong enough to overthrow Zeus. Zeus swallowed Metis to prevent her from having a second child. Metis did not die. She was immortal. Zeus only trapped her inside his body.

Months later, Zeus had a bad headache. He did not know what was causing the pain. Zeus went to his son Hephaestus (he-FESS-tuhss) for help. He asked Hephaestus to cut his head open with an ax. They then could see what was causing Zeus' headache.

Metis had given birth to Athena while she was trapped inside Zeus. When Hephaestus did as Zeus asked, Athena leaped out of Zeus' head. She was fully grown and fully clothed when she appeared.

This Roman sculpture was made around A.D. 300. It shows Athena (left) helping Prometheus (right) make people.

ATHENA'S WISDOM AND GIFTS

Athena's wisdom often helped gods as well as people. Zeus put the Titan Prometheus (proh-MEE-thee-uhss) in charge of making creatures to fill the world. In some myths, Prometheus went to Athena for advice on how to complete his task. Athena helped Prometheus shape people and animals out of clay.

Ancient Greeks believed Athena invented many things. They believed Athena created ships and chariots for people. Chariots were two-wheeled carts pulled by horses. Chariots carried soldiers into battle.

Athena protected heroes. She often gave them advice or gifts to help them on their quests. She helped Jason build the ship *Argos*. Jason sailed this ship when he went in search of the golden fleece. The golden fleece was the wool from a golden ram killed for Zeus. Myths say *Argos* was the largest ship ever built.

The Iliad tells about the last year of the Trojan War. During the war, Greek soldiers used a hollow, wooden horse to hide in and sneak into the city of Troy. Giovanni Domenico Tiepolo's painting shows people pulling the Trojan Horse into Troy.

Ancient Greeks and Romans told many types of myths. Explanation myths, like the myth of Arachne, explained why things happened.

Creation myths described how the world and the gods were created. These myths told of Athena's birth and how Zeus became ruler of the Olympians. The Greek poet Hesiod (HESS-ee-od) was famous for writing down creation myths. Around 750 B.C., he wrote *Theogony*. This book was the first collection of creation myths.

Quest myths are about heroes. Heroes performed nearly impossible tasks in these myths. Quest myths encouraged people to work hard to reach their own goals. Homer wrote down important quest myths in his two books *The Iliad* and *The Odyssey*. Homer was a Greek poet who lived around 800 B.C. In his books, Athena helps Greek heroes like Odysseus.

The blind Cyclops searched for Odysseus and his men.
But they tricked him. Jacob Jordaens' painting shows the men
hiding under sheep as they crawled out of the Cyclops' cave.

THE ODYSSEY

The Odyssey tells of Odysseus' adventures on his journey home after the Trojan War. Odysseus was king of the Greek island of Ithaca.

On his way home, Odysseus and his crew came to the land of the Cyclopes (sye-KLOH–peez). These one-eyed giants were the children of Poseidon (poh-SYE-duhn). Poseidon ruled the seas.

Odysseus hoped to befriend the Cyclopes. But one of the giants trapped Odysseus in a cave and killed several of his men. To escape, Odysseus blinded the Cyclops (SYE-klahpss). This act angered Poseidon. Poseidon created storms to keep Odysseus from sailing home.

Odysseus had many adventures as he tried to return to Ithaca. He fought several monsters. His crew was killed. His ship was destroyed. But he still struggled to reach his homeland.

Eventually, Athena asked Zeus to help Odysseus. Zeus then told Poseidon to let Odysseus return home. After ten years, Odysseus' journey finally ended.

The people of Athens built a temple to honor Athena.
They built the Parthenon on the Acropolis, a hill near
Athens. Part of the Parthenon still stands today.

Attica is an area of southern Greece. The people in this region honored both Athena and Poseidon. These gods often argued over who should be in charge of Attica's capital city.

The Olympians decided to settle the argument. Athena and Poseidon would each give the people of Attica a gift. The god who gave the most useful gift would earn the honor of being Attica's patron god.

Poseidon's gift was a horse. The people of Attica could use the horse to plow their fields, to ride, and to pull wagons.

Athena gave an olive tree. The oil from this tree's fruit would help cook food and light lamps. The tree also provided wood and food.

The Olympians judged that the olive tree was the most useful gift. Athena became Attica's patron goddess. The people of Attica named their capital city Athens in her honor.

Rene Antoine Houasse's painting shows Athena chasing Arachne. Athena stopped Arachne from harming herself and turned her into a spider.

ARACHNE

According to myths, Athena was the world's best weaver. But a woman named Arachne said she could weave better than Athena. People from all over Greece came to see the heavy pieces of cloth she wove. These tapestries were covered in beautiful pictures and patterns.

Athena heard of Arachne's bragging. She disguised herself as an old woman and visited Arachne. When Athena praised her work, Arachne said she could weave better than Athena. Her words angered Athena. Athena dropped her disguise and challenged Arachne to a weaving contest.

During the contest, Arachne wove a picture that made the gods look foolish. Athena became even more angry. She told Arachne that she had insulted the gods. Arachne felt bad after realizing what she had done. She wanted to kill herself.

Athena decided to save Arachne from harm. Athena turned Arachne into a spider. As a spider, Arachne used her weaving skills to make webs.

This statue shows Athena holding
the winged goddess Nike. In battle,
Nike led the way to victory.

20

MYTHOLOGY TODAY

Ancient Greek and Roman myths still influence the world today. A popular shoe company uses Nike's name. This winged goddess showed gods and heroes how to be victorious in battle. In art, she often is shown with Zeus or Athena. These gods never lost a battle because of Nike.

The myth of Arachne influenced how scientists named some animals. The name Arachnida is used for the group of animals that includes spiders, scorpions, and ticks.

Artists often use mythical figures in their art. Artists have created sculptures and paintings of Athena. Authors have written books about mythical stories. *Ulysses*, by Irish author James Joyce, is based on Odysseus' adventures.

Today, people no longer believe that Greek and Roman myths are true. Instead, they use science to explain things. But people still tell myths. Myths include interesting and enjoyable stories. Myths also help people understand ancient cultures.

Adriatic Sea

•Rome

ITALY

N
W • E
S

•Troy

GREECE

Aegean Sea

ITHACA

Thebes

Athens

DELOS

Ionian Sea

Sparta

KEY

• City

🏛 Oracle of Delphi

⛰ Mount Olympus

▨ Region of Attica

CRETE

Mediterranean Sea

SCALE
Miles
0   100   200

0   100   200
Kilometers

WORDS TO KNOW

ancient (AYN-shunt)—very old

culture (KUHL-chur)—a people's way of life, ideas, art, customs, and traditions

Cyclops (SYE-klahpss)—a giant with one eye in the middle of its forehead

immortal (i-MOR-tuhl)—able to live forever

Olympian (oh-LIM-pee-uhn)—one of 12 powerful gods who lived on Mount Olympus in Greece

overthrow (oh-vur-THROH)—to defeat a leader and remove the person from power

patron (PAY-truhn)—someone who gives help to a group of people

quest (KWEST)—a journey taken by a hero to perform a task

tapestry (TAP-uh-stree)—a heavy piece of cloth with pictures or patterns woven into it

Titan (TYE-ten)—one of the giants who ruled the world before the Olympians

READ MORE

Green, Jen. *Myths of Ancient Greece.* Mythic World. Austin, Texas: Raintree Steck-Vaughn, 2001.

Richardson, Adele D. *Hercules.* World Mythology. Mankato, Minn.: Capstone Press, 2003.

23

USEFUL ADDRESSES

The Parthenon Museum
Centennial Park
Nashville, TN 37201

Ontario Classical Association
2072 Madden Boulevard
Oakville, Ontario L6H 3L6
Canada

INTERNET SITES

Track down many sites about Athena.
Visit the FACT HOUND at *http://www.facthound.com*

IT IS EASY! IT IS FUN!

1) Go to *http://www.facthound.com*
2) Type in: 0736816089
3) Click on "FETCH IT" and FACT HOUND
   will find several links hand-picked by our editors.

Relax and let our pal FACT HOUND do the research for you!

INDEX